Love is a single rose.

Marriage is a garden.

Presented To

On The Occasion Of

On This Day

From

Love & Marriage

A book of humorous & heartwarming
comparisons between love & marriage
to make you smile,
even laugh out loud.

By Brenden Blake

Love & Marriage

Love is a newly formed bud.
Marriage is a full bloom.

Love comes in
passionate pink.
Marriage is golden.

Love is finding a flower.
Marriage is the whole garden.

Love finds a perfect rose.
Marriage finds the thorns.

Love is an introduction.
Marriage is the next chapter.

Love is never having to say,

"I'm sorry."

Marriage is having

"I'm sorry"

tattooed on your forehead.

Love is valuing another person.

Marriage is knowing

the exact cost.

Love is a many splendored thing.

Marriage is many shopping trips.

Love is the answer.

Marriage is all questions.

Love & Marriage

Love is when two people
become one.
Marriage is when they try to figure out
which one.

Love conquers all.
Marriage just surrenders.

Love is intoxicating.
Marriage is sobering.

Love is when you don't answer
phone calls during sex.
Marriage is when you return
phone calls during sex.

Love is finding happiness.
Marriage is keeping it.

Love is open to anyone.
Marriage requires a license.

Love is an asset.
Marriage is a tax deduction.

Love begets marriage.
Marriage forgets
important dates.

Love is getting to first base.
Marriage is coming home.

Love & Marriage

Love is when you ask
your partner's opinion
before you make a decision.
Marriage is when you ask
your partner's opinion
after it's already been made.

Love and war, all is fair.
Marriage, it's not.

Love is a quest.
Marriage is an inquest.

Love is true.
Marriage is truth.

Love is an affair.
Marriage is serious business.

Love is blind.
Marriage is 20/20 vision with
a magnifying glass.

Love looks
through a telescope.
Marriage looks
through a microscope.

Love is to admire with the heart.
Marriage is to admire with the
soul and spirit.

Love & Marriage

Love is kind.
Marriage is kin.

Love is kind.
Marriage is kindling.

Love is getting all dressed up.
Marriage is a bathrobe
and slippers.

Love is a fabric
that never fades.
Marriage is a pair of faded jeans
that have been
through the wash.

Love comes at
first sight.
Marriage comes before
first insight.

Love is a state of mind.
Marriage is when you are
out of your mind.

Love is a
sensation of the heart.
Marriage is heartburn.

Love makes a home.
Marriage furnishes it.

Love & Marriage

Love entails
change.
Marriage gets you into
big bucks.

Love is a beautiful story.
Marriage is an old movie
on television.

Love is a game with either
two winners or two losers.
Marriage is a tie.

Love quickens the senses.
Marriage stiffens the sinews.

Love makes you think
as much of another person
as you think of yourself.
Marriage makes you
think again.

Love is the milk
of human kindness.
Marriage is non-dairy creamer.

Love thy enemies.
Marriage can make a few.

Love is springtime.
Marriage is mealtime.

Love & Marriage

Love is when you
return something you can't afford.
Marriage is when you
charge it.

Love is open toed high heel pumps
and wingtips.
Marriage is two pairs of
tennis shoes.

Love is an evening out.
Marriage is an evening in.

Love is a word.
Marriage is a sentence.

Love is the leading
cause of marriage.
Marriage is the leading
cause of divorce.

Love is expectations.
Marriage is exceptions.

Love is dating.
Marriage is debating.

Love can be
easy to catch.
Marriage can be
difficult to diagnose.

Love & Marriage

Love makes
the world go around.
Marriage makes
your head spin around.

Love is a dream.
Marriage is waking up.

Love is holding hands.
Marriage is holding hearts.

Love is what
binds two people together.
Marriage is what
keeps sticking.

Love is accepting the other
person for who they are.
Marriage is making them the
person you want them to be.

Love is a prelude.
Marriage is the finale.

Love is music to the ears.
Marriage is domestic harmony.

Love is easier
done than said.
Marriage is easier
said than done.

Love & Marriage

Love makes people wonder if
there is sex before marriage.
Marriage makes people wonder if
there is sex after marriage.

Love can be hard to find.
Marriage can be hard to avoid.

Love is to be given away.
Marriage is to be kept forever.

Love is when you
give little gifts.
Marriage is when you
give in.

Love is when your
cup runneth over.
Marriage is when you get
a bigger cup.

Love is courtship.
Marriage is marksmanship.

Love is best.
Marriage is for
better or worse.

Love is like chess.
Marriage is the end of the game
when you are mated.

Love & Marriage

Love is finding your partner's
little habits funny.
Marriage is trying to
get rid of them.

Love is passion.
Marriage is compassion.

Love is like a song.
Marriage can make you
play second fiddle.

Love is overlooking mistakes.
Marriage is having them
pointed out.

Love passes quickly.
Marriage drags out.

Love thy neighbor,
but consider,
Marriage with someone
from out of town
who doesn't
know your family.

Love is the Fourth of July.
Marriage is a fifth.

Love is fireworks in an open field.
Marriage is a fire in the fireplace.

Love & Marriage

Love comes in on
little cat feet.
Marriage comes in on
muddy dog paws.

Love is intoxicating.
Marriage is a hangover.

Love is a many splendored thing.
Marriage is even more
shopping trips.

Love is like the wind.
Marriage is wearing a
windbreaker.

Love stays up all night.
Marriage goes to bed early.

Love is 12:00 A.M.,
January 1st.
Marriage is a few hours later.

Love is a symphony.
Marriage is your
favorite song
on the radio.

Love is a subject many
songs are written about.
Marriage is not.

Love & Marriage

Love is spending the afternoon
together, grocery shopping.
Marriage is picking up groceries
by yourself, on the way home.

Love springs eternal.
Marriage pounces.

Love is something
you fall into.
Marriage is something
you fall off of.

Love is eternal.
Marriage just seems like it.

Love & Marriage

Love is a banquet.
Marriage is not having to
make a reservation.

Love is breakfast in bed.
Marriage is eating out.

Love is a hot fudge sundae.
Marriage is a Sunday with nuts.

Love is espresso cappuccino
with cinnamon and
whipped cream.
Marriage is cocoa
with mini marshmallows.

Love & Marriage

Love is taking
your partner out.
Marriage is taking
the garbage out.

Love is a picnic.
Marriage attracts a(u)nts.

Love is a candlelight dinner.
Marriage is microwaved.

Love is swift
like the wind.
Marriage sits on the couch,
watching TV.

Love & Marriage

Love is a journey.
Marriage needs to stop
and ask for directions.

Love comes unseen.
Marriage has flashing lights
and a siren.

Love is a two-seater convertible.
Marriage is a mini-van.

Love is drifting along
in a canoe.
Marriage is being upstream
trying to find the oars.

Love & Marriage

Love begets love.
Marriage begets kids.

Love is over the moon.
Marriage can happen over a son.

Love forms bonds.
Marriage brings little dividends.

Love is when
one and one
makes a couple.
Marriage is when
one and one
makes two, and one to carry.

Love is having some
money left at the
end of the month.
Marriage is having some
month left at the
end of the money.

Love can be electric.
Marriage is usually charged.

Love is the ringing of bells.
Marriage is the wringing of bills.

Love is tender.
Marriage needs tenderizing.

Love comes when
you least expect it.
Marriage comes when
you are expecting.

Love is a shower of affection.
Marriage is prone to dry spells.

Love is a fire.
Marriage is a smoke detector.

Love, people like to
talk about their own.
Marriage, people like to
talk about someone else's.

Love is heaven on earth.
Marriage is made
in heaven.

Love hurts.
Marriage heals.

Love is magic.
Marriage is miraculous.

Love is given freely.
Marriage is priceless.

Love is giving.
Marriage is forgiving.

Love & Marriage

Love is wonderful.
Marriage is full
of wonder.

Love is to forgive.
Marriage is to forget.

Love is romance.
Marriage is romantic.

Love is an introduction.
Marriage is the rest of the story.

Love is you and me.
Marriage is us.

Love & Marriage

Love is patient and kind;
love is not jealous or boastful;
it is not arrogant or rude.

Love does not
insist on its own way;
it is not irritable or resentful;
it does not rejoice at wrong,
but rejoices in the right.

Love bears all things,
believes all things,
hopes all things,
endures all things.

– 1 Corinthians 13:4-7 (RSV)

Love & Marriage

Marriage is too.